DEDICATION

This book is dedicated to the descendants of our Gandy Dancers.

ACKNOWLEDGMENTS

Jim Oelschlager

Mike Blanc

Kristin Blackwood

Kurt Landefeld

Paul Royer

Jennie Levy

Sheila Tarr

A. Van Jordan

VanitaBooks, LLC

The Gandy Dancers
and Work Songs from the American Railroad
VanitaBooks, LLC

Text by Vanita Oelschlager
Illustration and design by Mike Blanc

Hardcover Edition ISBN 978-1-938164-08-8   Paperback Edition ISBN 978-1-938164-07-1

VanitaBooks.com

Huh!

the GANDY DANCERS

and Work Songs from the American Railroad

WRITTEN BY

VANITA OELSCHLAGER

WITH SPECIAL CONTRIBUTOR

A. VAN JORDAN

AND ART BY

MIKE BLANC

AMERICA'S RAILROAD

The early railroad became a sign of hope to the American people. People who worked on the railroad were doing very dangerous work. They found a great deal of support in each other and were a very close group. They were men of great honor.

The steam locomotive barreled onto the American landscape in the 1830s. A steam engine worked by adding wood or coal to a firebox and heating water in a boiler. This steam caused by the boiling water would propel the train forward. Early American railroads carried both passengers and cargo across the country. Early train lines went from Pennsylvania to New York and from Ohio to Baltimore. Railroad freight charges were much lower than other modes of transportation such as canals and turnpikes. This caused a great "railroad fever" to spread across the United States very quickly. Nine thousand miles of track had been laid by 1850.

Rocket   Lightning

Early railroad men took great pride in their locomotives. They were made of bright colors, ornate brass details and even featured painted scenes. The best thing a railroad could advertise was its speed. Early locomotives had names like *Rocket*, *Lightning*, *Velocity* and *Cyclone*.

Cyclone

Velocity

312

By the year 1910 the railroad employed 1,699,420 Americans.

They worked as conductors, brakemen, firemen, engineers, porters, telegraphers, switchmen, and in section gangs.

The conductor was the representative of the railway company. He was an awesome figure who had the ultimate say in the running of the train cars when they were out on a trip. He would often be referred to as the captain. He collected tickets from passengers.

The porters carried luggage and supplies aboard and were responsible for passenger care and comfort. As trains became the popular way to travel, this service industry, and especially the *Pullman Porters,** grew increasingly important.

The brakemen had possibly the hardest work. Early trains needed to be stopped by hand. This was the difficult task of the brakeman. He stood on top of the freight cars and turned a wheel to stop the train.

The fireman's job was not to put out fires, but to keep the fire going by throwing logs or coal in the firebox. They need to create the steam to keep the train moving. The engineer decided how fast the train could

*Pullman Porters were a select group of African Americans working for the Pullman Palace Car Company. In the 1860s, following the Civil War, they rose out of slavery to become dedicated workers, leaders of African American culture and trailblazers for the Civil Rights Movement in the United States.

go and still remain on the tracks safely. The telegrapher was able to wire or call ahead to the next town to communicate when trains would pass through.

The switchmen were responsible for the safe passage of trains through the stations. They could also signal ahead if there was a problem, like a runaway train. At times, there were many trains and people in stations and it was his job to keep the trains running on the correct tracks.

Some of the hardest working men on the railroad were those in the section gangs. They did the manual repairs and switching of the tracks. This was hard and dirty work. Men needed to be very strong.

From these hardworking section gangs came the Gandy Dancers and the songs they sang that helped keep them working together.

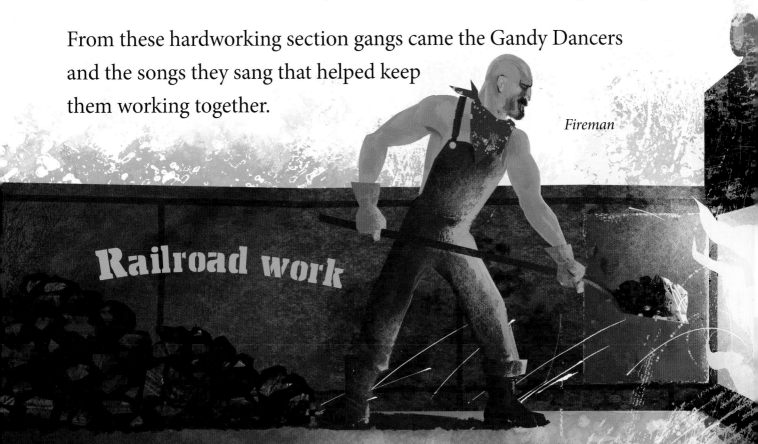

Fireman

Railroad work

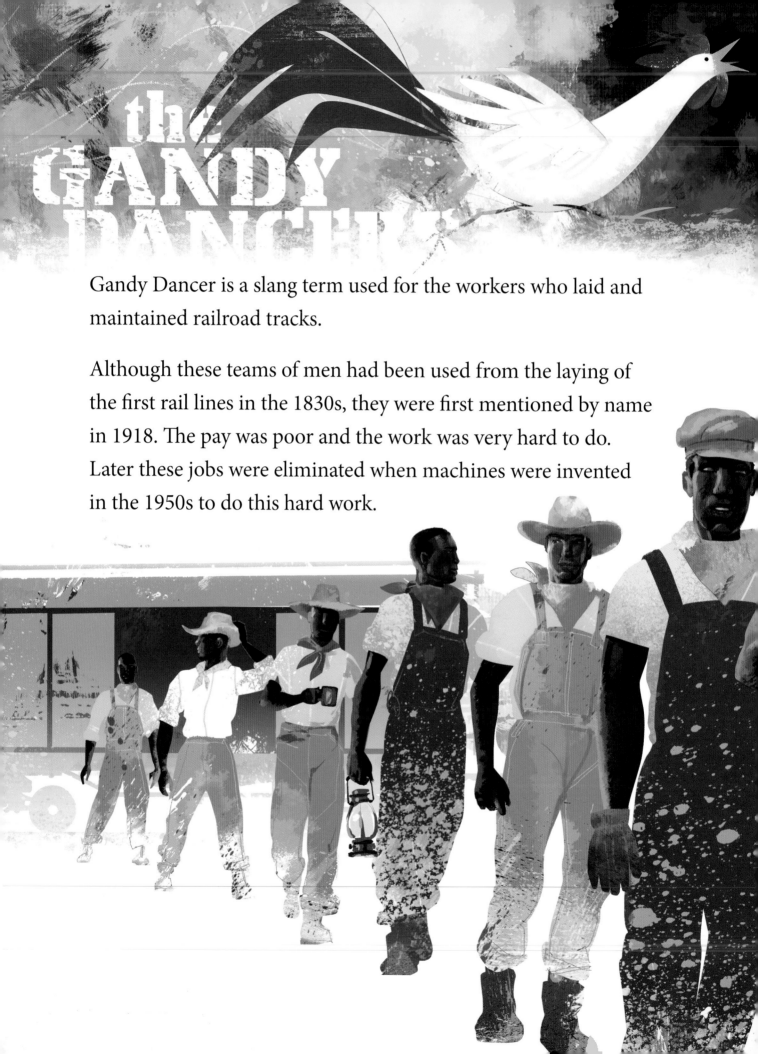

the GANDY DANCER

Gandy Dancer is a slang term used for the workers who laid and maintained railroad tracks.

Although these teams of men had been used from the laying of the first rail lines in the 1830s, they were first mentioned by name in 1918. The pay was poor and the work was very hard to do. Later these jobs were eliminated when machines were invented in the 1950s to do this hard work.

Cock a doodle do! Let's go to work!

No one is sure where the Gandy Dancers got their name. There may have been a "Gandy Shovel Company" or a "Gandy Tool Company," that may have been in Chicago. It could have made tamping bars, claw bars, picks and shovels.

A Gandy Dancer is a rail worker who moves track and tamps down the earth between ties on the rails. And this tamping caused a motion that looked as if the workers were dancing.

One Gandy Dancer described the tool as a large spoon with no flat end.

The workmen used a straight pry bar with a rounded top sharp end called a lining bar. They would just place the sharp end of the bar at a right angle to the track and step forward, pull up on the pry bar, and move the track. Crews of eight or more men would do this work. This was hard work and they had to push against the track many times to get it aligned the right way. This repetition was where the songs and chants came into play.

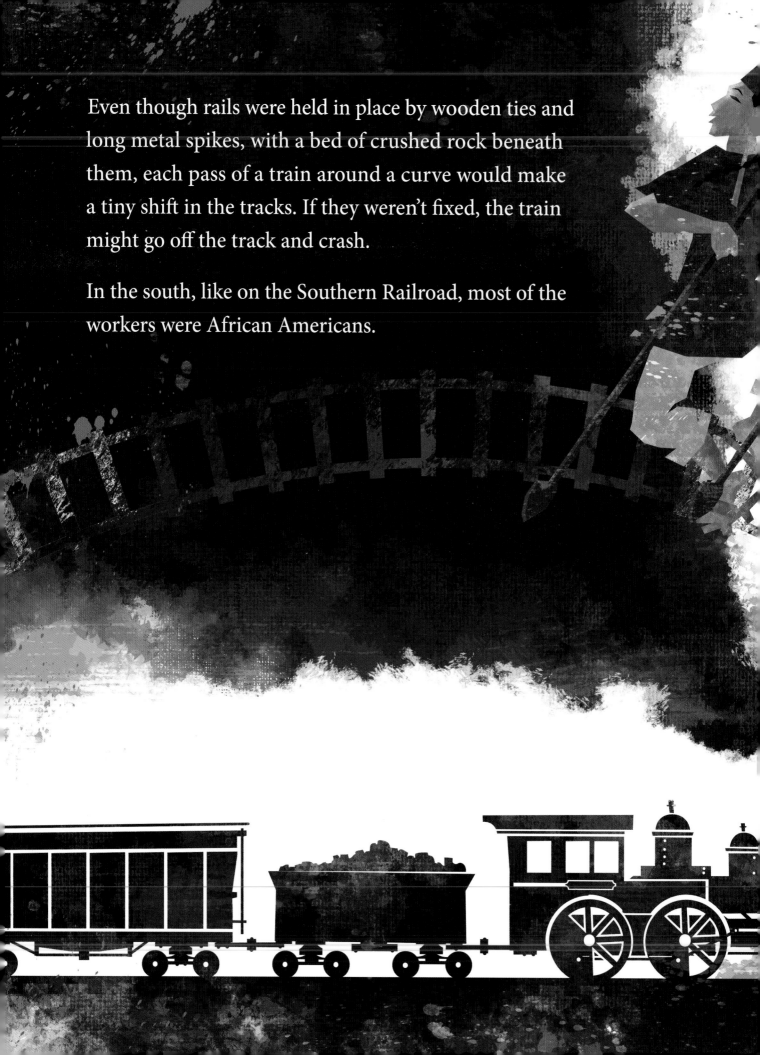

Even though rails were held in place by wooden ties and long metal spikes, with a bed of crushed rock beneath them, each pass of a train around a curve would make a tiny shift in the tracks. If they weren't fixed, the train might go off the track and crash.

In the south, like on the Southern Railroad, most of the workers were African Americans.

In other parts of the country crews were made up of recent immigrants and other minorities who wanted steady work despite poor wages and working conditions.

The Chinese, Mexican Americans and Native Americans were in the West. The Irish were in the Midwest, and Eastern Europeans and Italians in the Northeast laid and maintained track as well.

Though all Gandy Dancers sang railroad songs, the African American workers were always using song to coordinate work. Their songs for this were mostly chants. The workers made up songs to help them all push harder and at the same time. The sound the men made when it was time to push was, "Huh!"

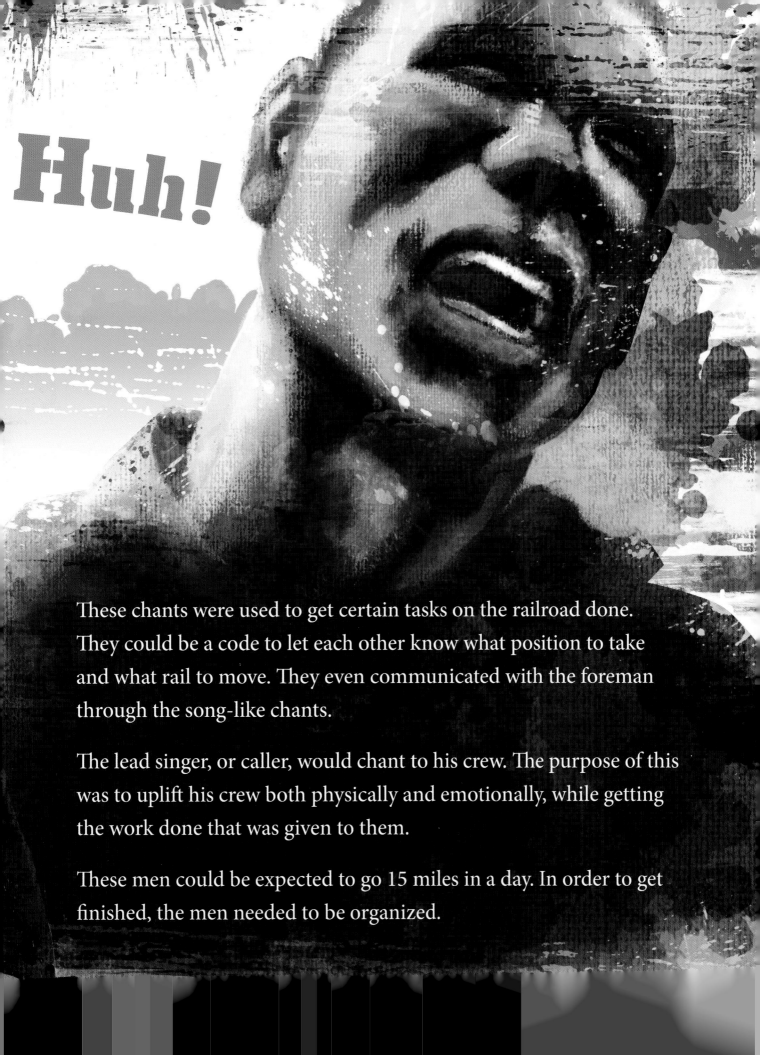

Huh!

These chants were used to get certain tasks on the railroad done. They could be a code to let each other know what position to take and what rail to move. They even communicated with the foreman through the song-like chants.

The lead singer, or caller, would chant to his crew. The purpose of this was to uplift his crew both physically and emotionally, while getting the work done that was given to them.

These men could be expected to go 15 miles in a day. In order to get finished, the men needed to be organized.

Here is an example of a chant. Remember when you see the word "*Huh!*" that was when each man was to push the rail.

Up and down this road I go
Skippin' and dodging a 44
Hey man won't you line 'um . . . Huh!
Hey man won't you line 'um . . . Huh!
Hey man won't you line 'um . . . Huh!
Hey man won't you line 'um . . . Huh!

Well I've been out East
And way out West
I believe I like
Alabama the best.
Been out East . . . Huh!
Been out West . . . Huh!
I think I like . . . Huh!
Alabama the best . . . Huh!

Hey man won't you line 'um?

And here is another one that is a little shorter.

> I had the St. Louis blues . . . *Huh!*
> I'm just as blue as I can be . . . *Huh!*
> I had the St. Louis blues . . . *Huh!*
> I'm just as blue as I can be . . . *Huh!*

It is said that one lead singer was able to go all day long and not repeat a song!

Following are some of the songs that were probably used by the lead singer to help workers work together.

Alan Lomax was inspired by the Gandy Dancers and their chants to write *Skip to My Lou*.

SKIP TO MY LOU

Begin with Chorus:
Lou, Lou, skip to my Lou
Lou, Lou, skip to my Lou
Lou, Lou, skip to my Lou
Skip to my Lou, my darlin'!

Lost my partner, what'll I do
Lost my partner, what'll I do
Lost my partner, what'll I do
Skip to my Lou, my darlin'!

Chorus

I'll find another one, prettier, too.
I'll find another one, prettier, too.
I'll find another one, prettier, too.
Skip to my Lou, my darlin'!

Chorus

Can't get a red bird, blue bird'll do.
Can't get a red bird, blue bird'll do.
Can't get a red bird, blue bird'll do.
Skip to my Lou, my darlin'!

Chorus

Flies in the sugarbowl, shoo, shoo, shoo.
Flies in the sugarbowl, shoo, shoo, shoo.
Flies in the sugarbowl, shoo, shoo, shoo.
Skip to my Lou, my darlin'!

sugarbowl, shoo, shoo, shoo!

Here is another one you might have heard.

SHE'LL BE COMIN' ROUND THE MOUNTAIN

She'll be comin' round the mountain when she comes
She'll be comin' round the mountain when she comes
She'll be comin' round the mountain,
She'll be comin' round the mountain,
She'll be comin' round the mountain when she comes.

She'll be drivin' six white horses when she comes
She'll be drivin' six white horses when she comes
She'll be drivin' six white horses,
She'll be drivin' six white horses,
She'll be drivin' six white horses when she comes.

Oh, we'll all go

out to meet her . . .

Oh, we'll all go out to meet her when she comes

Oh, we'll all go out to meet her when she comes

Oh, we'll all go out to meet her,

Oh, we'll all go out to meet her,

Oh, we'll all go out to meet her when she comes.

We'll be singin' "Hallelujah" when she comes

We'll be singin' "Hallelujah" when she comes

We'll be singin' "Hallelujah,"

We'll be singin' "Hallelujah,"

We'll be singin' "Hallelujah" when she comes.

This American favorite has an important 'back story'. A back story is a story behind the story. First, you'll read the song about a man who hated slavery. Then, you'll learn the back story.

JOHN BROWN'S BODY

John Brown's body lies a mould'ring in the ground
John Brown's body lies a mould'ring in the ground
John Brown's body lies a mould'ring in the ground
But his soul goes marching on.

Sing the chorus:

Glory, glory, Hallelujah!
Glory, glory, Hallelujah!
Glory, glory, Hallelujah!
His soul goes marching on.

He's gone to be a soldier in the army of the Lord
He's gone to be a soldier in the army of the Lord
He's gone to be a soldier in the army of the Lord
And his soul goes marching on.

Chorus

Glory, glory, Hallelujah!

JOHN BROWN
DIED
1859

John Brown died that the slave might be free
John Brown died that the slave might be free
John Brown died that the slave might be free
But his soul goes marching on.

Chorus

The stars of heaven are looking kindly down
The stars of heaven are looking kindly down
The stars of heaven are looking kindly down
On the grave of old John Brown

Now, for the back story.

It is said that in 1861 Julia Ward Howe visited a Civil War army camp. She heard the men singing *John Brown's Body* to the tune of a camp-meeting hymn called *Say, Brothers, Will you Meet Us?* Deeply moved, she later wrote *The Battle Hymn of the Republic* to that tune. That song became the marching song of the northern armies.

Let us die to make men free.

THE BATTLE HYMN OF THE REPUBLIC

Mine eyes have seen the glory of the coming of the Lord;
He is trampling out the vintage where the grapes of wrath are stored;
He hath loosed the fateful lightning of His terrible swift sword;
His truth is marching on.

> *Chorus*
>
> Glory, glory! Hallelujah!
> Glory, glory! Hallelujah!
> Glory, glory! Hallelujah!
> His truth is marching on.

I have seen Him in the watch fires of a hundred circling camps;
They have builded Him an altar in the evening dews and damps;
I can read His righteous sentence by the dim and flaring lamps;
His day is marching on.

> *Chorus*

I have read a fiery gospel, writ in burnished rows of steel;
"As ye deal with my contemners, so with you my grace shall deal;
Let the hero, born of woman, crush the serpent with his heel,
Since God is marching on."

> *Chorus*

He has sounded forth the trumpet that shall never call retreat;
He is sifting out the hearts of men before His judgement seat;
Oh, be swift, my soul, to answer Him! be jubilant, my feet!
Our God is marching on.

> *Chorus*

In the beauty of the lilies, Christ was born across the sea,
With a glory in His bosom that transfigures you and me;
As He died to make men holy, let us die to make men free,
While God is marching on.

> *Chorus*

Here is a popular American folk song about a
railroad worker escaping from a prison work crew.

TAKE THIS HAMMER

Take this hammer . . . *Huh!* – carry it to the captain . . . *Huh!*
Take this hammer . . . *Huh!* – carry it to the captain . . . *Huh!*
Take this hammer . . . Huh! – carry it to the captain . . . *Huh!*
Tell him I'm gone . . . *Huh!*
Tell him I'm gone . . . *Huh!*

If he asks you . . . *Huh!* – was I runnin' . . . *Huh!*
If he asks you . . . *Huh!* – was I runnin' . . . *Huh!*
If he asks you . . . *Huh!* – was I runnin' . . . *Huh!*
Tell him I was flyin' . . . *Huh!*
Tell him I was flyin' . . . *Huh!*

If he asks you . . . *Huh!* – was I laughin' . . . *Huh!*
If he asks you . . . *Huh!* – was I laughin' . . . *Huh!*
If he asks you . . . *Huh!* – was I laughin' . . . *Huh!*
Tell him I was cryin' . . . *Huh!*
Tell him I was cryin' . . . *Huh!*

I don't want no . . . *Huh!* – cold iron shackles . . . *Huh!*
I don't want no . . . *Huh!* – cold iron shackles . . . *Huh!*
I don't want no . . . *Huh!* – cold iron shackles . . . *Huh!*
Around my leg . . . *Huh!*
Around my leg . . . *Huh!*

I was cryin' . . .

Yonder lies a steel drivin' man.

One of America's great railroad ballads recalls the legend of John Henry, the mighty steel-driving man. His story is a heroic battle between men at manual labor and machines in the new age of industrial automation. Over time a great many versions of John Henry have collected more than 20 verses. This one selects several to summarize his tale. Here is the musical score for piano and vocal.

JOHN HENRY

Ami.   C   C+⁶

beat me down, (F) I'll die with a ham-mer in my
three in-ches down, and he died with his ham-mer in his
cap-tain and said, "Ain't nothin' but my ham-mer suck-in'
rail - road tracks, So he could hear the trains go rumb-lin'
by — his — grave, they say, "Yonder lies a steel — driv-in'

Emi.   F+⁶   Cmaj.⁷F+⁶ C

hand, Lawd, Lawd! Die — with a ham-mer in my hand."
hand, Lawd, Lawd! Died — with his ham-mer in his hand.
wind, Lawd, Lawd! Nothin' but my ham-mer suckin' wind."
by, Lawd, Lawd! Hear — the — trains go rumb-lin' by.
man, Lawd, Lawd! Yonder lies a steel — driv-in' man."

Modern day poets are still inspired by the chants that were used
by the Gandy Dancers. A. Van Jordan is one of those poets.
The following two poems come from the book *Rise*.

Excerpt from

JOHN HENRY TELLS ALAN LOMAX ALL ABOUT THE WORK SONG THE NIGHT BEFORE HE RACES THE STEAM DRILL

John Henry, can you give me an authentic work song to record?

Jinte on back there, give me some more.
Jinte hard now and let it roll.
Nod your head, Shorty — you' almost out the door.

Jinte on down and put her on the floor.
Give it to me now and watch her stroll.
Jinte on back there, give me some more.

Now you don't want ole Sally to think you're a bore,
So Jinte on down there, tonight you gonna jelly roll.
Yeah, nod your head, Shorty; you' almost out that door.

On your way to Sally's arms out on the dance floor.
Boy, that gal sure got a pretty little mole.
Jinte on back there, give her some more.

VANITA OELSCHLAGER is a wife, mother, grandmother, philanthropist, former teacher, current caregiver, author and poet. She is a graduate of the University of Mount Union in Alliance, Ohio, where she currently serves as a Trustee. Vanita is also Writer in Residence for the Literacy Program at The University of Akron. She and her husband Jim received a *Lifetime Achievement Award* from the National Multiple Sclerosis Society in 2006. She won the Congressional *Angels in Adoption*™ Award for the State of Ohio in 2007 and was named *National Volunteer of the Year* by the MS Society in 2008. She was honored as 2009 *Woman Philanthropist of the Year* by the United Way of Summit County. In May 2011, Vanita received an honorary Doctor of Humane Letters from the University of Mount Union. In 2013, Vanita joined *The LeBron James Family Foundation* to serve on its Advisory Board.

MIKE BLANC is a graphic artist and illustrator of countless publications for both corporate and public interests worldwide. Mike's work with author Vanita Oelschlager includes children's titles; *Francesca, Postcards from a War, I Came From the Water, The Pullman Porters*, and *Bonyo Bonyo, The True Story of a Brave Boy from Kenya* with associate artist Kristin Blackwood.

A. VAN JORDAN is a poet and the Henry Rutgers Presidential Professor of English Literature and Creative Writing at Rutgers University-Newark.

DONATION. VanitaBooks donates all net profits to charities where "people help people help themselves." Ten percent of all net profits from this book will be donated to *Friends of Writers*, a not-for-profit 501(c)(3) organization that enriches American poetry and fiction by cultivating new and vital literary voices that reflect the entire nation. It supports the students, alumni and faculty of its partner, the Warren Wilson College MFA Program for Writers. Learn more online at www.wwcmfa.org/friends-of-writers/.

the GANDY DANCERS

and Work Songs from the American Railroad

To Do

Why don't you try one yourself? Read the others over and see if you could do that. Write it about your pet or anything else in your life.

Here is an example for you.

BILLY BLUE

I had a dog named Billy Blue
Oh the things that dog could do
Old Billy Blue . . . *Huh!*
What he could do . . . *Huh!*
Old Billy Blue . . . *Huh!*
What he could do . . . *Huh!*

Go on! Try it! This is a way to help us always remember those great men of the railroad . . . the Gandy Dancers. They knew that hard work is easier when we all work together. And don't forget to sign your work so we can remember you.

Vanita Oelschlager

The Gandy Dancers are not around now. The world moved on and that job is gone. Just like the Pullman Porters, the Gandy Dancers were an important part of history. This book will help you to never forget these great men and the songs that powered their work.

RESOURCES

READ MORE ABOUT AMERICA'S RAILROAD

Children's Nonfiction

We Were There at the Driving of the Golden Spike by David Shepherd and William K. Plummer

The Incredible Transcontinental Railroad: Stories in American History by R. Conrad Stein

Trains by Matthew Harper

The Pullman Porters: an American Journey by Vanita Oelschlager

Children's Fiction

Until the Last Spike: the Journal of Sean Sullivan, a Transcontinental Railroad Worker by William Durbin

The Iron Dragon Never Sleeps by Stephen Krensky

On the Blue Comet by Rosemary Wells

The Boundless by Kenneth Oppel

For Teachers

Irish Gandy Dancer: a Tale of Building the Transcontinental Railroad by Ryan Michael Collins

The Iron Road: an Illustrated History of the Railroad by Christian Wolmar

GO ONLINE AND LEARN MORE

www.encyclopediaofalabama.org

LEARN FROM A REAL GANDY DANCER

earthstonestation.wordpress.com

WATCH A FILM ON GANDY DANCERS

Gandy Dancers 1973 by Jack Schrader and Tom Burton.

You can find this wonderful video from **folkstreamer** on YouTube.

'Round the circle
> hands like wind.

Shouters' spines
> held straight.

Shouters' heels
> swing the floor.

The faith in the circle
> is the circle.

The spirit in their eyes
> sings in their soles.

A woman shouts
> from her knees;

her hair sweeps moonlight
> from shouter's feet.

Then they sing:
> "aaah, girl, go lowerer, lowerer."

She raises up:
> shouters sing:

"rise from the mire, higherer, higherer"
> as a fieldhand's shadow

springs from the floor.

A. VAN JORDAN

Also by A. Van Jordan
M-A-C-N-O-L-I-A, Quantum Lyrics, and The Cineaste

SHARECROPPERS, RING-SHOUTERS AND STARS

Stars are of little value
in the hands of a sharecropper.
It's the sun that dresses him in the morning,
the baptism of his throat with water
that gets him through the day,
the moon playing along the edges
of his wife's hair
that brings him home at night.
At night, once a week, she leads him to the church;
they are God-fearing folks;
in the circle, their boots
shuffle spirit around the room:

> *The rhythm builds and*
> > *the rhythm breaks.*
>
> *They "shout" in twos or*
> > *they "shout" in fours.*
>
> *Their shoulders "hock";*
> > *the heads snap back.*
>
> *The toes shuffle;*
> > *the heels stomp.*
>
> *Off to the side*
> > *hands a'clappin'.*

Shake that rail!

Shake that rail sweet as a apple core.
Steel ain't nothin' but a woman, so give her some soul.
Nod its head, Shorty; you almost out that door.

Jinte on down, boy, what you draggin' for?
Better git in there before they paddy roll.
Jinte on back there, give me some more.
Nod your head Shorty — get on out that door.